T0196985

OPEN DOORS

VERTA VERTALEOSO

WESTBOW
PRESS®
A DIVISION OF THOMAS NELSON
& ZONDERVAN

WestBow Press books may be ordered through booksellers or by contacting:

WestBow Press
A Division of Thomas Nelson & Zondervan
1663 Liberty Drive
Bloomington, IN 47403
www.westbowpress.com
844-714-3454

All Scripture quotations are taken from the King James Version.

ISBN: 978-1-6642-0586-4 (sc)
ISBN: 978-1-6642-0585-7 (e)

Print information available on the last page.

WestBow Press rev. date: 11/30/2020

On one side of the door is my dog who loves me. On the other side of the door is where I stand. The only thing stopping us from being together is the door between us. I can tell my dog wants to be with me, as bad as I want to be with her, by the way she is scratching and whining at the other side of the door.

I may even be calling my dog's name because I want to be with her, but that is still not opening the door allowing us to be together.

While all I need to do is open the door allowing my dog and I to be together, and while it is what we both want, opening the door takes action on my part. It is that simple. All I must do is open the door and let my dog in. What comes to my mind is that Jesus is knocking on the door to your heart. He is softly calling your name. Will you answer his calling you to himself?

In Revelations 3:20, "Behold I stand at the door and knock; if anyone hears my voice and opens the door, I will come in and will dine with him, and he with me." Opening the door to your heart for Jesus is as easy as it gets. Simply open the door and he will come into your heart.

In Acts 16:31 scripture says, "And they said, believe in the Lord Jesus Christ and thou shalt be saved, and thy house." Believe, open the door to your heart and ask him in. Please do it today, without delay. Jesus is the only way.

Jesus is a gentleman. He will not come into your heart unless he is invited. When he enters your heart there is no other kind of pure and perfect joy ever felt by anyone this side of Heaven. Once the Lord enters your heart, you will be happier with him, than without him. You will never want to be without him again.

Revelations 3:20
Acts 16:31

CONTENTS

HIDE AND SEEK

My friend has the most beautiful cross that she wears around her neck. It has sentimental value. More than that, it has diamonds in the middle of it. It is beautiful. It stands for the cross her Savior hung on. She never takes this cross off. It stays proudly worn.

Lately I have noticed a sad thing. When she hangs around her new friends, she tucks the cross in her shirt so no one can see it. The friends she hangs around with do not think there is anything cool about being a Christian, so she hides her Christianity from them too.

One day she was in a hurry while getting ready to meet one of her new friends and she forgot to tuck her cross into her shirt. When she met up with her friend, they could not help but notice the cross due to its beauty. When asked about it, my friend hid the cross and denied she was a Christian, saying it was just an old piece of costume jewelry.

How often do we as Christians do what my friend did? We hide Jesus from others by what we do and say, or by the places we go. When angry, we say things or do things that Jesus would never want us to do. Things that God's word clearly tells us not to do. We may even go to places that can only lead to the beginning of our destruction. We act like we do not even know Jesus.

In the Bible, Peter a devoted disciple of Jesus denied him in front of others. Later he was sorry for it and told Jesus he was sorry.

Jesus forgave him because Jesus still loved him despite any sin he had committed.

So, there is hope for us just like there was for Peter. If you have ever found yourself hiding Jesus, the one who died for you, you can be forgiven. Jesus loves you and shows mercy and grace towards you. Repent, go and sin no more.

John 3:16 says, "For God so loved the world, he gave his only begotten son, that whosoever believeth in him shall not perish, but have ever lasting life."

FATHER ON EARTH AND IN HEAVEN

For reasons I choose not to go into, I was always running away from home in my teenage years. I would return home but then run away again. My Mother grew weary of my running away. One day after I returned home, I knocked on the door to our house. After opening the door, my Mother refused to let me in the house She informed me I would have to speak to my father before I would be allowed in the house. My father was in one of our outbuildings. I turned and left my Mother, which left me stinging from rejection. I walked down the little path that led to the building my father was in. What would he say to me? What would he do when he saw me? I was afraid but desperate. I wanted to turn back. I did not want to face my father. If my Mother was so angry with me as to turn me away, how must my Father be feeling?

I cautiously opened the door. My father did not hear me enter. His back was to me. I saw him there with his green Army coat on, working on one of his small motors. I took one step closer to my father and stopped. He still did not know I was there. I stood there for a moment watching him. When I got the courage, I quietly spoke to him simply asking, "Dad?"

My Father turned around and looked at me. As he walked towards me there were tears in his eyes. I stood there quietly. When my father was close enough, he stretched both arms towards me and without hesitation he hugged me, and I hugged him. Oh, how I love my Father. How good his hug felt that day after being on the streets. He then spoke softly to me saying, "I'm glad your home. I have been praying you would come back home."

I told him how Mother would not let me in the house. My father told me to follow him and we headed back up the path that led to the housel. When we got to the house, he opened the door for me, and we walked in together. My mother seeing us together said not a word. I will never forget that day as long as I live. I will never forget how it looked, how it felt, to see, and be in my Father's wide-open arms.

When I grew older and remembered that day, I knew in my heart of hearts that, that is what it will be like when we see Jesus. Despite what we have or have not done, Jesus will forgive us and will welcome us into Heaven with arms wide open while giving us a Heavenly hug, and hearing, "Well done thou good and faithful servant." Matthew 25:51

I cannot think of a better analogy for the biblical story of the prodigal son, (Luke 15:11-32) than the way my dear, precious, Father welcomed me home that with his arms wide open.

CHORES

There are rust spots all over my car that need repairing. I bought everything needed to do the repairs and to do them right. I stored the equipment in our garage.

There is a huge hornets' nest in the corner of our house outside. I even bought what I needed to rid ourselves of the potential danger of getting attacked by hornets. I stored the equipment in our garage.

I love my flower bushes that line up along our long driveway. With those beautiful bushes come responsibilities. They need to be trimmed and tied back to keep their beauty from getting in the way of visitors using the driveway. I bought what I needed to tie back my bushes. I stored the equipment in our garage.

There are more projects needing to be done. There was equipment bought and stored in the garage. We had all the tools we needed, but the tools would do us no good if we never took them out and used them. It is that way with us and our Bible which is filled with the tools we need to get

When we ask Jesus in our heart, it opens the door to Heavenly tools just waiting to be used. Tools that can be used in our life as well as the lives of those we loved and those we have never even met. One of the biggest and best tools we have, is our bible. Our bible leads us and guides us, providing the tools we need.

It is exciting to read 2 Timothy 3:16-17 and to realize the bible was given to us as an inspiration of God. We can and should use the word of God in correction and instruction in righteousness. We are to use our bible as tools to teach us what is right and what is wrong in our lives.

CHANGING FACES

There's a toy that has a face on the body of a cartoon character. On this toy there is also a button located on its side, that when pushed in, changes the face of the toy. So, while you may start out with a frown, if you push in the button the face goes around and around. You choose when to stop it and you end up with a different face. You can go from a frown to a smile in just a few seconds. You could go from a smile to a frown in seconds as well. It was fun being able to change the faces so quickly we change our sadness to happiness, in just a few seconds. Then to, what if we could change our angry face into a pleasant looking face, in just a few seconds? But why can't we I asked myself. Why can't we go from angry to pleasant in just seconds?

After thinking for just a few short seconds I quickly figured out that we cannot change the looks on our faces as quickly as that toy because there is something getting our way. What is it that keeps getting in our way? It's our feelings. Yes, our own feelings. Our feelings are all that stands in the way of changing our world or that of someone else's for the better. We get angry and don't want to let go of whatever it was that made us angry in the first place. We have a hard-enough time letting go of our anger in days let alone in seconds. Then what about when we are sad? Whatever it was that made us sad, begins to hang heavy on our hearts. It weighs us down, yet we begin to feel uncomfortable in our frown. How can we get rid of the weight that causes our face to turn from a smile to a frown in only seconds?

Okay so maybe we can't do like the toy does and turn things around in just seconds. Maybe we need time to process and cool off before we can manage a complete face change. But just think about it. Think about how much time we would save if we just let feelings of disappointment, anger, or any other negative go feeling go and change those negative feelings into feelings of delight, happiness, and joy so many other positive feelings. Our face reflects our feelings. Have you ever tried to smile when you are angry, or hurt, or severely disappointed? Can that even be done?

Everyone must search his or her own heart. I cannot do it for you nor can anyone else do it for you. In reading Ephesians 4:26-27: Proverbs 10:12: we find We should be angry yet sin not. We are reminded that hatred stirs up conflict and we are not to hold grudges. I pray the Holy Spirit lead you into changing your frown into a smile in sixty seconds or less.

3 + 1 = 1

How did I ever come up with my 3 + 1 = 1 equation? My son who was a single father of two young girls, and the stepfather to two older girls. He also held down one full time job, and two part time jobs. With him being the only contributor to the household expenses getting paid, he was always juggling finances, yet everything always seemed to have gotten paid and the girls' needs were always met.

Through word of mouth he came across a job making more money than he was making at the time. This young man went through the hiring process including an interview. He later found out he was not selected for the position and was somewhat disheartened by it.

My son was not discouraged so much that he gave up improving his career. As time went on another position became available that was even better than the one before. His reputation went before him as a man of integrity. It seemed like forever before he heard what he longed to hear. He had been offered the position and he happily accepted it. He was told he was selected based on his great physical ability as well as his ability to seemingly balance his three jobs. A feat not many people are able or willing to do. Because of the three jobs, he accrued a great deal of diversified experience. One of those jobs was of a military position, another a police officer position, and the third was a Probation Officer working with offenders who were often violated, arrested, and taken to jail.

Because of his three jobs he was chosen for the one job. 3 + 1 = 1. When you think about it, it's like that for us in our relationship with our Savior. 3 + 1 = 1. Number 1 being God, the Father, the source of all things, who gave his only son, Jesus, number 2, who sent the Holy Spirit, number three to dwell in each of us. When we ask Jesus to come into our heart, we become his sons and daughters. One big happy family. All three of them living in us as one....

Everyone must search his or her own heart. I nor anyone else can do it for you. After reading John14:26, and II Corinthians 13:14 I pray the Holy Spirit lead you into all understanding.

CHOICES

At this time in my life I find myself being disabled. Because of the diseases within my body, I am no stranger to daily pain which tries to ruin my life. I am determined to try my best to rise above the pain and to carry on through life as though I am well.

I am use to someone helping me out around the house. Whether they be disabled and living with us or not, it helps me out quite a bit. Recently my husband developed a pain in his leg. After tests and medication, he was still in pain. Medications that left him tired and weak ended up not helping him with the pain. All three of us were struggling with our own demons due to pain.

I grew tired of the many piles of laundry sitting aside waiting for someone to take care of it. I also had a grocery list a mile long needing to be picked up from two different stores, because of different items being on sale.

I knew my husband was unable to help out, so I asked my disabled daughter to help me with it. The laundry needed to be done at the laundry mat due to our washer being out of order. After telling my daughter to help, she took one look around and asked that she be left at home. I was beside myself in disbelief thinking how she did not want to help me. I sat alone wondering if I should force her to go and suffer her bad reaction at having to help, or should I tell her she does not have to help? After a time of silence, I decided to give her a choice thinking she would surely choose to help, due to not wanting her ailing mother to do all the work alone.

Imagine my surprise when once given the choice, she opted out of helping me. I had to do it all on my own. But could I? Yes, I could but at what price? While at the laundry mat, I had to work very slowly while often having to sit down until the pain in my body let up. This made it take forever before getting it done. By the time I got done with the laundry, I still had the groceries to get. I fought back the tears, not wanting anyone to see me cry. However, by the time I was done with the groceries, there was no holding it back. The tears flowed freely when getting home, and I fell onto my bed grabbing my medication. It took several hours before I felt like living again.

Often when someone is given the chance to choose between right and wrong, they end up doing the right thing in a much more pleasant frame of mind. Forcing someone to do the right thing may not end up in a good way.

It is that way between us and God. He is not a God who forces us to accept his son as our Savior. He does not force us to do good. He does not force us to help others. He does not force us to do anything. God gives us choices on where we want to spend eternity, who we want to serve, and who we want to help. He gives us choices every day on how we want to see things, or who we want to love, and to help and to be there for us. He allows us to make bad choices even if it means hurting someone we love in the process or being selfish to those who cannot fend for themselves, whether young, or old, sick or well. We do better when given a choice and God knows that. He does not want a bunch of robots or puppets serving him. He gives you the choice of going to heaven or hell. He does not send you to either one. You choose for yourself where you want to go. He lets you go where you choose.

Jesus is there for you if choose to ask him into your heart. Jesus is there for you when facing decisions should you ask him for advice on what to do. Jesus is there for you when you are sick and need his help to feel better. Matter of fact, there is nothing on Earth Jesus will not help you with if you ask him. It is your choice. I pray you choose to ask Jesus for help in doing what is right, while making decisions, and how to react to people you come in to contact with.

John 3:16 tells us how God loves us. You can have eternal life along with your friends and family.

TOOLS

One of my precious granddaughters was going to school for nursing. She was a wonderful Christ follower who wanted to be a Christian in every part of her life. Not just what people saw but even in things no one saw. She was over visiting us one day when she stated she needed to go to the ATM machine, and she would be right back. When she returned, she came to the door and mentioned she had a problem. She proceeded to tell us she had locked herself out of her car with her keys in it. Both my husband and I followed her out to her car and for the next hour and a half we tried to get into her car to unlock it. We did not have the right tools needed to get into her car. We tried all kinds of things to get the job done with what we had. Our granddaughter climbed on top of her car and tried to pry open her sunroof hoping to gain access that way. This did not work so I climbed into her car hoping to gain access by pushing down the back seats which would allow someone to climb in the car, but That did not work either.

My dear husband was trying this whole time to get to the lock button inside the car with a metal hanger. After trying all these ideas, we realized it was not going to work but we could not give up because she had to have her keys to get home. We had no choice but to continue to work on getting into the car. We just did not have the right tools.

My granddaughter called her boyfriend and told him what

happened and asked for him to come over and help her out. He of course agreed to come right away. Minutes later he showed up all prepared and willing to help.

After an hour and a half had passed, a neighbor who lived right across the street came by with tools in his hands. He had seen us struggling and asked if he could help. We answered in unison yes of course he can help. He made one or two attempts and got a different tool. After a few tries he did indeed get into that car and, he unlocked it, and was able to her in her car. Everyone was happy to have the car opened finally.

First of all, no one had any tools. What could you do if you needed tools to get the job done but had no tools? You could not get done what you needed without the tools.

Second, imagine yourself in this position, locked out of your car with no tools. Someone shows up with exactly the kind of tools you need to get in the car and you say no, I am not going to use your tools. Just go away mister, I do not want your tools or your help. How good would that be? Of course, you are not going to turn away the man who has the tools to get you in your car. Not only does this guy have the tools you need, but he is even willing to do the job for you.

First of all, once again, you are thinking why anyone in their right mind would turn away the man who has the right tools and who is willing to do the job for you. But I know of millions of people who do that every day of their lives. It is people who turn away from Jesus. People who do not have the tools to live a moral life, and they struggle every day to make the right decisions, because either they do not have the tools at all, or they have the wrong kind of tools.

And then again secondly, there are millions of people who hear of Jesus. They hear of all the ways or tools, Jesus has, to help them live not only a good moral life, but a Godly life. A Godly life that will lead them straight into the kingdom of God when they pass from this life to the next. But as Jesus stands there with all the tools, waiting to help, he is told to go away.

If you want to get the job done here on Earth, trusting in Jesus, living a good life, which leads to a life of eternity, then you need Jesus. Jesus has all the teachings you need. Jesus is here to help you. Please do not turn him away. He will not only help you in your everyday life, but he did the job of securing a place for you in heaven, for eternity by dying on the cross for your sins. He carried the weight of your sin and death on his shoulders for you so you would not have to.

Please do not try to live without Jesus. Please do not turn him down as he calls you by name. He offers you a better life here on Earth. He offers you an indescribable life of heaven for eternity. Please do not turn him away. Allow Jesus to help you get the job done. Ask Jesus into your heart. When you ask him into your heart, everything Jesus owns becomes yours too. Why would anyone turn Jesus away? He has everything you could ever need." For I know the plans I have for you, declares the Lord, plans for welfare and not for evil, to give you a future and a hope." Jeremiah 29:11

THE UNHAPPY ALIEN

Many years ago, a movie came out about an alien wanting to go back home. He had been left here by accident and immediately began searching for ways to get back home. You never see his home, but you know it is up beyond the stars, and beyond Earths' ability to get there. He was uncomfortable being so far away from home. He longed to be home and was biding his time until he could return to the place that held his heart.

Eventually He gets a bunch of people from Earth to help him figure out a way to get home. He had all the right tools, but he had to use them. If he did not use the tools to build a spaceship he would never get to go home. So, he used the tools he had, built a ship, waited for the right time and went home.

He was welcomed home by family and friends alike. He was finally where he was supposed to be. He never fit in on planet Earth. Earth just never compared to home. On Earth he did not act like Earth's residents, he had his sights set on going home and he studied how to get home. He was determined to get home and once returning home he remembered why he fought so hard to get home. Home was where his heart was.

We too should be so determined to reach home. Heaven. We are just passing by here. Home is where our heart is. We should have the desire and determination that the alien had and use tools we have, to guide us home. Our sight should be set on Heaven. We should be using our tools with the goal being Heaven, and while we wait for that time, we need to learn to live like we are citizens of Heaven.

The Bible is our tool in which we use to get to know Jesus. Jesus is the way. He is the way the truth and the light. You can only make it home through Jesus. We do not have to build a ship to get to our home beyond the stars. Jesus takes us there. When Jesus is ready, he will come for us.

We do not work to get home. We cannot get home by our own works. Jesus already did the work for us when he died on the cross for our sins. The work has all been done. Once we were lost but now, we are found.

Sometimes daily living can be a very tiring thing. We get tired and maybe we even act in ways we should not due to our being weak if only for the moment. Jesus said when we are weak, he is strong. Let Jesus be your strength, for he alone is the way the truth and the light. John 14:6

OH NO NOT AGAIN!!!

As a child I had a favorite movie that only came on once a year. Every year I looked forward to seeing it. My Mother grew tired of seeing it repeatedly, year after year. Not me. I loved it and I did not care if I had already seen it one hundred times, I was ready to see it one hundred times more.

No matter how old that movie gets, no matter how many times I have seen it I still love that movie. So, think of your favorite movie. No matter how many times you have seen it, you still want to see it every now and then, right? How about the age of your all-time favorite movie? It doesn't matter how old it is, it remains your favorite. What about the stars in your favorite movie? They must be getting every bit as old as the movie itself. To this day my favorite movie makes me feel all warm and fuzzy inside just from the old memories watching the movie brings to the surface.

It should be like that in our relationship with Jesus. No matter how old God's word is, no matter how many times you have read the bible, or one certain verse, and maybe even memorized one certain verse you never grow tired of reading it over and over. It still means as much to you as it did the very first time you read it. It's still alive. If it's a story in the bible that you love reading, you have the main character or even the seemingly insignificant character, that you want to read about. You have Your Favorites that make you feel all warm and fuzzy inside.

We have all been there when we just aren't like our happy old self and we just can't put our finger on why. Then because of the hope or promises the bible gives us we begin to feel much. much better. It is because the bible brings us so much comfort and peace that we desire to spend more and more time reading it. We need to make sure we set time aside to read our bible every day.

Deuteronomy 31:8-9 John 16:33 Psalms 27:13-14 Isaiah 41;10, are just some of the comforting verses you will find in your bible.

FEAR

When I was a case manager working with high risk families of child abuse, I was conducting a home visit with one of the families I had been working with. I was monitoring the home for potential child abuse. This family appeared to be more violent than most of my clients. I met with my clients weekly, observing the interaction within the family members. I watched how the children settled in along with their parents. If there were pets in the home, it was always helpful to see how they treated their pets or how they played with their pets.

It was during one of these visits that I witnessed abuse. A young boy kicked his dog in the ribs from one side of the room to the other. The boy was a rather large six-year-old who for some reason found it necessary to overpower and abuse the family pet. Of course, the situation concerning the boy was identified and steps were taken to get the boy the help he needed and to be sure the family dog never suffered such a kick or abuse again.

I rescued this dog from the dangerous situation it was in. After explaining how important it was to provide a safe environment for the family pet to live in, and how important it was to teach children how to treat the family pet, I suggested it may be necessary to rehome the dog to prevent any injury to the dog. Perhaps the family could try again with another dog once the boy becomes a little older.

After more discussion on safety issues for the dog and child, the parents agreed it would be best to rehome the dog and asked if I would agree to help them do so. I did agree to removing the dog and took her with me at the end of the home visit.

The dog went home with me until such a time I could take her to the pound. She had the saddest looking eyes I ever saw in a dog. It did not take but a few hours for me to fall head over heels in love with her and to feel the need to protect her from any further harm in life. We as a family adopted her and named her Lovey because she was shown mercy and love, when removed from a home that was abusive. One of the most noticeable behaviors I noticed with Lovey, was her fear of storms. Before we could even hear the thunder from the approaching thunderstorm, Lovey could hear it, and immediately began to shake all over. Sometimes she would find a place to hide where no one could see her. Lovey was terrified of storms and was moved by this fear. After taking her to the Vet, it was determined she needed the assistance of medication to calm her down.

Much like our precious pup, we too have fears that need to be faced. We can become so fearful that it turns into terror. We can also allow such fear to rule our reactions to the thing we are fearful of. Think for a moment of how you would feel having to face your worse fear head on. Would you run from the situation and steer clear of it? Do you avoid facing your fears at any cost? Do you run to Jesus at the first sign of becoming afraid, or do you run to him as a last resort when there is nothing else to do?

Jesus understands our being afraid of things that could come to us in life. He speaks about fear in his word. He gives us encouragement and strength to face what may lie ahead for each one of us. His word is his speaking to us and is always there for us.

In Deuteronomy 31:8 we are assured he will never leave us nor forsake us, and we are encouraged to not be afraid or discouraged. Romans 8:28 as well as 43:1 encourages to fear not for we have been redeemed.

PATSY THE PUP PUP

I was eating my dinner in our living room while room watching a baseball game with my husband. Patsy my canine baby was next to me watching my every bite. My other dog was on his way over, hopeful of getting some cuddle time. He never begs for food but instead for cuddle time with me. My Pup Pup was threatening to attack him due to the food she thought was up for grabs. I did not want her to hurt the other dog, so I scolded her and tapped her gently on her fanny. I have a no spank rule for my canine babies so if they ever do anything that warrants a light tap on the fanny it is quite an Earth-shaking ordeal. So, after receiving the light tap on the fanny she backed up and moved away from me. I could not stand the separation under these circumstances, her thinking I was mad at her. She looked so sad with her head slightly hanging down and watching me from afar. I immediately forgave her, got up and walked over to her giving her a great big hug, while telling her I loved her and forgave her. She then rested her head on my shoulder and took a deep sigh. All was well in her little world.

This scenario reminds me of my relationship with God. I depend on God for everything I do. I need God to provide what I need throughout my life. I need the love of God. God comforts me when I am down, and I feel a since of cuddling between my God and I.

When I do something wrong, I may feel a sense of separation

between God and I. The bible states how our iniquities have made a separation between us and God. However, in Romans 6:23, it tells how God sent his son Jesus to redeem us.

When I repent for my wrongdoing, our relationship is restored. While I may have hung my head in despair, once I have repented, any sadness over my wrongdoing, begins to fade and I am restored to right standing with my Father in God.

Remember John 3:16 "For God so loved the world he gave his only begotten son, that who so ever believeth on him shall not perish, but have everlasting life."

MEMORIES OF A LIFETIME

I was watching an old black and white movie with well-known stars in it. These stars were in the prime of their life. They appeared to have everything. They appeared in good health, good looks, money, fame, and fortune. They had everything anyone could ever want out of life it seemed. They had to be feeling on top of the world. I hope they gave time for themselves to enjoy all the things they worked so hard for. Yet after all these years, where are they now? They are all dead. Some of the names of these people are not even known by the generation of our time. They do not get to be movie stars in Heaven or Hell. They are just spirits like those that were once living and not, movie stars. Their bodies are in the grave just like everyone else's who have passed away.

Everything we have obtained here on Earth according to Matthew chapter eight will wind up where moth and rust will corrupt or even for thieves to steal. Stardom in Hollywood is only for a short time here on Earth and nothing more.

If we all concentrated on obtaining things that are laid up in Heaven for us the world might be a better place.

Whether you are at work or at home, you and I should be Heavenly minded. Store up your treasures in Heaven. The Lord will keep your rewards safe. Your rewards will be waiting for you. Reading Matthew 6:19 – 20 will bring you strength and direction.

The old movie stars of years and years ago have had their

Earthly rewards, big mansions, worldwide recognition, and fortune. However, as the bible states, these rewards will, and have already fall prey to corruption. I wonder what our world will be like if all the Hollywood stars stored up as much Heavenly treasures, as they have Earthly treasures. Again, according to the bible, if that were the case, their treasures would be waiting for them, unlike now where all the Earthly treasures are gone.

OUT OF LOVE

I was diagnosed with a disease that was not terminal but was a sentence for a lifetime of pain and suffering. It is known as the suicide disease due to the high level of pain with little to no relief. I couldn't really say I grew use to the pain, but I grew accustomed to it. I learned how to go through life doing the things I wanted or needed to do until the pain became intolerable. When I reached that point, I could only lie down, take my medication, and cry while waiting for some relief to come.

My husband was and is a great support for me. He loves me and it shows in the way he cares for me. There was a time in his life when he lived in constant pain due to something pinching a nerve causing significant pain, making it very difficult for him to even stand. He suffered that way for what seemed like an eternity while insurance and I fought over authorization for a much-needed MRI.

After a time of his living with pain, his MRI was finally approved. I accompanied him to the appointment and got in line to get registered. I could see by his shifting from leg to leg and by the look on his face that he was in pain. While I was standing in line with him both of my legs began hurting. I couldn't stand to see him in such pain. Not even thinking of my already aching legs, I got him to take a seat in a chair nearby. The look of relief that shot across his face as he sat down confirmed that allowing him to sit was the right thing to do.

As the line moved ahead, the pain in my legs greatly increased. Part of me thought I must be crazy taking his place in line so he could sit, when I felt so much pain myself while standing. But I loved him. If I could take his pain from him if even for a few short minutes I would do it, and I did.

Not that I am in anyway to be compared to Jesus and all he has done for me and for everyone else on Earth, but I realized in some small way that I was being Christ like. The bible tells us to esteem others higher than ourselves. Philippians 2:3-5. Jesus Christ became a substitute for our sins. Jesus took our place, and suffered for us, so we would not have to suffer. The pain Jesus took upon himself while he hung dying on the cross was meant for us. He bore the pain and humiliation for us so we would not have to. He did this with no thought of saving himself. He hung and suffered on the cross for mine and your sins. Because he took our pain and sins, we can go to Heaven when we pass away.

He bore our griefs, our sorrows, and was crushed for our iniquities. Isaiah 53: 4- 6. Jesus bore our sins in his body. He died on the cross for our sins, because he loves us. 1 Peter 2:23 – 25.

DESTRAUGHT

I know a former friend who has several children. She made her children her life as they grew up. You might say when her children grew up and moved away from home, she had an attack of empty nest syndrome. She shared her heart with me many times. One incident especially stayed with me and caused me to begin to see into the heart of Jesus.

She was trying to maintain a close relationship with her children. She desperately tried to remain close to them. She also tried to never offend them but to be there for them and to be truthful with them. There was one daughter whom my friend loved very much, yet they seemed to have difficulties with keeping their relationship in good standing.

Their relationship got to be so strained, that there were periods of time where the beloved daughter did not talk to her mother. This greatly hurt my friend. She was desperate to have a good relationship with her much loved daughter, but it just was not working. It seemed like my friends' heart was breaking and she continued to be in tears when talking about the state of the relationship.

As I thought of what my friend was going through with her daughter, I wondered if God was anything like that in pursuing us. I wondered if we should be that determined in pursuing our relationship with God. How often do I spend time with the Lord?

Am I willing to forsake everything for a relationship with God? Am I willing to go the extra mile to spend time with God?

Jesus is pure and perfect and only has our best interest at heart. I had to ask myself since Jesus is ever present and ready to meet with us, am I making time to be with him? According to John Romans 10:17, we can have faith in God. Read it and find out how.

If given the chance, my friend would say, Daughter I love you with ever being of my heart. I am blessed to have you in my life, and when you become so angry with me, I feel an unbearable ache in my heart. Life is so short, and none of us are guaranteed the next morning. Please let's not waste the time we have left with hurtful, silent times between us.

BLACKIE

S he's a black dog with obvious trauma having taken place to her face. No one would honestly tell the facts regarding what happened to her. It must have been bad since it affected not only her left eye but also her left ear that is not able to stand up like the other ear.

Blackie is a dog filled with spirit and energy. She rarely felt the need for a nap and needed little rest. She would play for 24 hours straight if she could only find a play mate willing to do the same. Blackie demanded attention and adventure. She would paw at me until she got the attention she demanded. When she first arrived at our little rescue, she demanded adventure. She refused to submit to the safe boundaries of a fenced in yard. One night under the protection of the darkness she slipped out of the gate that had accidently been left open a crack. She was caught before ever getting out of the yard. She was saved from any potential harm.

There are many verses in the bible speaking of boundaries such as Ephesians 4 13 – 14, Romans 12:2 and many more. God sets boundaries for us not because he is some big mean God who does not want us to have any fun. God does not sit on his throne ready to bop us over the head when we cross the boundaries. He sets boundaries because he loves us and wants us to be safe and happy. The boundaries are meant to keep us within the perimeters of safety.

Like Blackie, the happy little puppy, we may cross the boundaries from time to time that God has set, and find ourselves in a mess. But God does not leave us there to fend for ourselves. Once we acknowledge our error, he picks us up and puts us on the right track.

After being dropped off at our house, Blackie did not want to stay at first. As time went on, she missed her former owner less and less and accepted the love and comfort we provided for her. She began to enjoy being with us. Much like Blackie, because of her spending time with us, and becoming closer to us and making peace with us, the more we spend time with the Lord, we will begin to love and appreciate being in his loving presence.

SALT

There was nothing like swimming in the creek on a hot Summer day. When I was but a young girl, I and the two neighbors that I swam with would build a dam and capture the water. It made the water waste high which was deep to us. It was usually myself, my sister, and different neighborhood kids who went swimming in that creek. There was a lot of splashing, dunking and fun being had when we all got together. There were no worries while swimming in the creek. Well, almost no worries. There was however one small thing that sometimes threatened our having a good time. It was the leeches. We tried to swim in the middle of the creek avoiding the creek beds. However, sometimes you just could not avoid them, and you found yourself playing right in the middle of the creek beds. Especially when you were playing a rowdy game of tag, or lazily floating down stream on a raft.

While finding a leech on your belly or between your toes could be a frightening thing, we had help in getting the leeches off. You dare not grab them and try to yank them off. They needed to be removed the right way.

Most of the time when we swam in the creek my mother went along with us. I remember how proud I was when everyone knew my mom was sitting nearby on the creek bank. She was the hero of all that swam in the creek that day. Some kids even cheered when she showed up. You see my mother brought with her the cure for leeches. It was a bottle of salt and a small first aid kit. All the kids liked her.

One day while swimming in the creek, someone found a leech on them. They were distraught. He tried to pull it off, but it had been there for a while and was firmly attached. He could not just yank it off as that was not the safest thing to do. I noticed the poor kids looking at the horrible thing so I ran right over and told him about my mom and what she could do. We both hurried over to her and it did not take long at all before after applying salt to the leech for it to drop off, falling to the ground. We were back swimming in no time. My mother being the hero once again.

Salt is mentioned in the bible. In Matthew 5:13 it states, "You are the salt of the Earth." I believe this means, in this world of evil and wickedness, we as Christians are to be encouraging, loving, peacemakers, doing our part to make the world a better place. We are to live as Christ did. He stood up for what was right and was not afraid to stand firm against wrong. He showed mercy and grace to those he came in contact with. It further states in the same verse, "But if the salt loses its saltiness, how can it be made salty again?" That may seem like a harsh thing to say, but in part it can simply mean we can no longer sit back and be inactive in building the kingdom of God. We are asked to work for the good of this world, and for the kingdom of God, by showing encouragement, peace, and most of all, love.

In Job 6:6, the first part of the verse asks us, "Is tasteless food eaten without salt?" How would it be if you salted your food, but the salt had lost its flavor? You might as well do without, as the salt is no longer any good and you would end up tossing it out. How would it have been if the salt my mother was using was no longer any good? It would have done nothing to remove the leech. So, if salt loses its flavor it may as well be tossed out. If we lose our zest for living for Jesus, and promoting righteousness, in love and mercy, we are doing nothing for the world or the kingdom of God.

It is my prayer and heart's cry, that in the midst of evil in this world, we as Christians remain steadfast in promoting godliness using love and mercy. We can with the help of the Lord, remain salty for Jesus.

NOTHING WRONG HERE

At the writing of this book my friend had only one son, and that only son is in his thirties. She had four lovely, and bright daughters and she has such great love for all her children.

In one way her daughters were easier to raise than her son. Whatever her daughters did once they become teenagers seemed mild compared to what her son put her through. He was not even doing anything wrong. He became a soldier in the United States Army, a police officer, and a Probation Officer working with criminals of all sorts. All way more dangerous occupations than what she had picked out for him. You see she wanted him to be minister, or a doctor in a nice safe environment.

All the while the son grew up, he never did anything wrong as far as she was concerned, or at least she does not remember anything. She only remembers him doing one good deed after another. Now, mind you his sisters may have a thing or two to say about that, but that is a whole other story.

In 1 John 1:9, Jesus talks about how if we confess our sins, he is faithful and just to forgive us.

Jesus not only forgives us of our sin, he says in Psalms 103: 12, he spreads them as far as the East is from the West.

What good parent walks around constantly reminding them of everything they have done wrong? They do not want their child living in their past sins. They want them to move forward. I believe

God loves each of his children and that includes you and I. I believe God sees us through the blood of Jesus, that was shed for our sins and we are wearing white robes of righteousness.

I heard a preacher say one time that when the devil points his finger and reminds us, and God, of what sins we have committed, that perhaps the Lord might reply to the accusing devil on our behalf by using scripture. In Hebrew 8:12 it says, "I will forgive their wickedness and remember them no more." In Matthew 18:22 it says we ourselves are to forgive someone 70x70. Would God do anything less than that? In Psalms 103:1. One of the things it says about Jesus is that he is slow to anger and is abounding in love for us. He carries our sins as far as the East is from the West. That is encouraging.

Let's remember Jesus died on the cross for you. He died a painful death so you could escape the punishment of hell. Do not let this opportunity of asking Jesus into your heart go by. He loves you, and once you ask him into your heart, he forgives your sins, remembers them no more and Heaven awaits you. John 3:16

HAVING YOUR SENSES ISN'T EVERYTHING

D espite her defects she is one of the smartest and well-behaved pups we have ever had the privilege of having. She was house trained quicker than any other pup we have trained. She has a deep sense of love for her humans that she lives with.

Just as we love our precious pup despite any fault she may have, Jesus loves us, despite our faults. Whether it is spiritual or physical it does not matter, he chose us, and he loves us. We do not have to be perfect, and none of us are. We can just be us and he loves us anyway.

Because of all the things she does despite her disability and because we are praying she receive her hearing and her sight which would be nothing but a Miracle, we named her Angel. Just as Angel runs to us when she is afraid or having a hard time, we can run to Jesus. When we go through hard times, no matter what they may be, he wants us to run to him so he may comfort us. We can freely put our trust in Jesus. Whatever we need he can provide. With God all things are possible. Matthew 19:26

Isaiah 41:10 is one of many scriptures to hang onto for our journey here on Earth. "So do not fear, for I am with you; do not be dismayed, for I am your God. I will strengthen you and help you; I will uphold you with my righteous hand. Seek Jesus through prayer and by reading the bible.

You may be finding yourself in unsure times causing fear to be in your life. Psalms 34: 4, says, I sought the Lord and he heard me, and delivered me from all my fears." Proverbs 18:10 assures us of our safety, "The name of the Lord is a strong tower: the righteous run into it and are safe."

There are many more nuggets in God's word just waiting for you to find it so it may strengthen and encourage you. Seek out Gods word and you will find the answers to whatever you need in life, no matter what it may be, since one of Gods promises are "Seek and ye shall find." Matt. 7:7&8.

THERE IS ALWAYS THAT ONE

I have long been familiar with the verse found in Matthew 18:12, however it was hard for me to understand how one could be just important as the 99.

When I was a young teenager, I became pregnant with my first child. I had all the excitement other mothers did when expecting their first child. What would we name it? Where do we put it? Can we afford it? What did my baby need, and did I have enough time to get everything my baby needed? I wondered what kind of parent I would be. Will it be a boy or a girl?

From the minute I found out I was carrying a baby it was all I focused on. It was all I wanted to talk about and think about. I was so excited. I planned and expressed my excitement every day to anyone who would listen.

No matter how excited I was, during the middle of my pregnancy, I delivered a still born baby. I felt such an emptiness from somewhere deep inside. Losing my precious baby changed everything. All the plans I had made. All the things I hoped for and planned for were never to be brought to realization. How could I just pick up and carry on like nothing had ever happened? How could I go on when my baby who was supposed to be with me, was gone.

One year later I gave birth to my second child. Then came the third, the fourth, and lastly the fifth. I had been blessed with five beautiful children and I showered them with much love and adoration. I was never sorry for one minute having had five children. Most families were satisfied with less than five but not I. I loved my children and they became my world.

Everything I did was for or because of my children. We went to Volleyball games and basketball games. We traveled wherever they went to watch our children participate in victory over the opposing team. We attended programs, concerts, and graduation ceremonies. We went camping together and drove to the next state to go swimming together. We traveled a short distance to an amusement park a few times, and even ate out for dinner with all five of our children. Our children were important to us.

At night we had devotions before bedtime. When I sent them to bed each night, I knew they were home safe and protected. I felt like a bird who covered her babies with her wings, protecting them from harm, allowing them to sleep soundly.

It was several years before the scripture in Matthew made any real sense. The way I figured, was the other ninety-nine that were left behind to go after the one, were safe and sound right where they were. The shepherd knows all is well with the flock and he could spend some time going after the one sheep.

I think the shepherd might have felt something was missing. Even though he had ninety nine other sheep to look after…..there was still that one that was missing. It was not to be forgotten. I know now, no matter how important my five children are to me, or no matter how much of my world they are, there would always be that one. Every bit as important was my first baby. Not to be forgotten was that one.

For anyone who has ever lost a baby, there will always be that one. It may not be in your arms, or may not be lying in their crib asleep, but it will always be that one. That one special child, that blessed little lamb, that you look forward to meeting someday.

THE FIGHT FOR A RIGHT

Recently my husband was at a nearby clinic and needed a certain test ran on him to determine the reason for continued pain. My husband was told he could not be treated until a diagnosis had been made. The only major symptom reported by my husband was pain. The longer he was left untreated without this test, the stronger the pain became. It was unbelievable but my husband's insurance refused to pay for the much-needed test that a specialist had ordered. My husband and our family were at a loss as to how to go about getting him the much-needed test. Even the specialist could not get the insurance company to budge.

When I got involved it became a bit nerve racking. I called the insurance company four days in a row attempting to get the insurance to authorize the test. I sat and watched my husband become depressed due to his great suffering and feeling like there was no hope in ever getting the test completed.

I explained to the insurance company that by refusing to authorize the test that was ordered by the specialist, they were preventing my husband from receiving a timely diagnosis and treatment where time may be of great importance. I emphasized that the fault in this delay lay squarely in their laps.

Another day of contacting the insurance company. This time I was told to have the specialist call them as soon as possible, however, no promises were made by the insurance company. I did as the insurance company requested, yet I was beginning to wonder if all I was doing was doing any good. I turned to prayer and then went about my normal business feeling I could do no more than I had already done.

Two hours later I received a call from the Specialist's office wanting to set up a time for the much-needed diagnostic test. The insurance company had finally approved the test. Both my husband and I were elated.

We were able to schedule the test for the very next day. We were finally able to have hope for an end to this pain and suffering. It took someone being an advocate for the patient to get the desired results. We too have an advocate. His name is Jesus. He is an advocate for us regarding God the father.

An advocate is someone in support of, in favor of, a promoter, protector, adviser, supporter, backer, recommender, of a cause. Jesus is our advocate in providing a way of escaping an eternity in hell by making a way for us to be forgiven and for us to abide with him in Heaven for eternity.

Jesus may make a particularly good example of an advocate for us since in John 3:16 he tells how much he loves us. In Philippians 4:19 it tells how God will supply all our needs. Psalms 18:2 tells us the Lord is our protector. It goes on to say with him we are safe. In Isaiah 9:7 we are told Jesus is our counselor. Even David in the bible tells us Jesus was his helper as found in Psalm 54:4.

There are many verses in the bible telling us all about Jesus and how he is our advocate in many ways. To sum it all up, verse Psalm 16:5 -11 simply tells us Jesus is our all in all, making him our everything.

Have you made the decision to allow Jesus to be Lord of your life? My hope and prayer is for you to study God's word and for you to decide to ask him into your heart, making him your all in all.

LITTLE RATTY

I love people and I love dogs especially Rat Terriers. I also love my family. With that being said, you may possibly understand the love I had for my RATTY. He was also known as Little Ratty and was named after my father, who is my greatest of all Earthly heroes.

Little Ratty was named after my father who is a veteran of the United States military. My father is a tough man who has seen a lot, and has had to do many an unpleasant things under the command of his higher ranking officer. But he was not only tough in his service to his country, he was tough outside the military as well. If something needed to be done you could count on him getting it done because my dad just got the job done no matter what.

We rescued Little Ratty, who was only a small puppy, from a very abusive home where he had either been in a fight with another dog or had wounds inflicted upon him by human hands. We found him abandoned in a garage, shivering in a corner. We took him home where he was babied and pampered like royalty, as we fell deeply in love with him.

It was only a week after we rescued him that Little Ratty became desperately ill with Parvo. Once again we rallied around Ratty giving him round the clock loving care. He slept with me through the night on a towel right beside my head so I could hear his every move or cry for help. Once again, with God's help and with the help of one of my oldest daughters, we were able to pull Jack through that horrible illness that has claimed many of puppy lives.

A few months later once Little Ratty became strong enough, it was time to do the responsible thing and get him neutered. I dropped him off at the Vet office and kissed him good-by and told him I would be back for him after his surgery. After dropping him off I went out to eat with my son. Just as we were given our food my phone rang telling I needed to return to the Vet immediately. It was then they informed me my Little Ratty did not make it through the surgery.

I was crushed and my heart was broken. I asked God why he would pull my Little Ratty through beatings and illness only to have him die on the operating table. I did not seem to get an answer from God, but to this day I have never forgotten about my Little Ratty.

As a mother I rescued my children as they were growing up from dangerous situations. Once I took four of my children out of state chasing after one of my children who was missing. She had left for a date with her boyfriend who we did not approve of. When she did not return home at the set time, we became worried for her safety. I became terribly upset and determined to find my beloved daughter.

Through a series of events like phone calls to many different people and many different agencies along with different police departments, I was able to find out she must be in a cabin somewhere in the state of Michigan. I also found out she was with three different males of different ages ranging from 13 to 50. I just knew my daughter would not have done this of her own free will. I trembled with fear as we made a call to the Michigan State Police. They were instrumental in us locating the small cabin where she was. Two state police accompanied us to the cabin on the lake. They carefully looked into each window to determine if there was any dangerous situation they may be walking into. My mother bear instinct had gotten us this far and we were about to get our daughter back safely.

I had rescued my five children out of many different situations that could have been dangerous. I was there for any of them for whatever it was they needed. When we become children of God, we have a God who protects us from things we are often not even aware of. There are times when we wish God would get us out of a bad situation a whole lot sooner than he does, but God is never late. God is always on time and in his time, which may be totally different from our time.

There are many times in the Bible where God protects those who follow him. The bible tells us we will face difficult times. The bible also provides us with many scriptures to comfort and protect us. For instance, in 2 Thessalonians 3:3, we read, "But the Lord is faithful, and he will strengthen you and protect you from the evil one." And in Psalm 34:19, "The righteous person may have many troubles, but the Lord delivers him from them all." There are many more wonderful scriptures regarding protection in the bible. Search out his word for wisdom and peace of mind. Even through rough times in our life we can turn to Jesus and his word for comfort and reassurance. I could not have made it through life this long had it not been for Jesus and his word, or the bible.

My prayer for you is that you too find comfort in knowing the Lord as your savior and turning to him for every one of life's adventures.

THE HUG

I was thinking of a loved one lost to our family not to long ago. I hate death with a passion. Death causes emptiness and loss of fellowship with those we love. My thoughts also go to my beloved parents who are both in their 80's. I thought about how much I love them and loved visiting them. I could not stand the thought of death separating them from me. My cousins have lost one of their parents and I can tell it has not been easy for them. My mother has helped me through my difficult first marriage. I ran to her with injuries both physical and mental as a result of that marriage. My mother offered words of encouragement when I suffered through a terrible disease. Then there was my father. Let me tell you about my father.

My father is a man's man. He knew pretty much everything you could know. If he did not know how to fix something, he learned how to do it and he fixed it himself. If he did not know how to build it he would study how to and then build it. He was a scuba diver. He helped our local law enforcement find dead bodies lost under water. He helped groups of people looking to fish for salmon by leading them to some of the best places to find them. He dove down into sunken ships finding small left behind treasures. He was a race car driver and he built his own race car. Not only did he race, but he won some of his races. I have memories as a young girl sitting in the bleaches watching my dad take the victory lap holding on to the checkered black and white flag as he proudly hung it out the window for all to see. On top of everything else my dad was a hard worker at anything he did. He often held down two jobs if not three to provide for his family making it possible for my mother to be a stay at home mom. He was a great provider for his family. He was that and so much more.

My father was not at home much as you can imagine hearing how busy he was. When he was home if we were good, we had nothing to worry about. He watched television with us, bought snacks for us, and he would get his guitar out and sing to us. However, if we were misbehaving for my mother while he was at work than we had much to fear. My father was a firm believer in using discipline to get his point across. I hated being afraid of my father coming home when I had been misbehaving because I loved him so much and I wanted our time together to be filled with fun not regrets.

One thing I especially can tell you about is my father's hugs. Even to this day when I visit him the first thing I do is get my hugs from my mother and father. While my mother's hugs are nice, nothing can compare to getting a hug from my dad. His hugs simply put are out of this world. His hugs leave me feeling loved, safe and protected like all is going to be alright. His hugs give me a sense of home. Yet in all of that my father's hugs are strong and steady. I hug him at the beginning of our visit and at the end of our visit which leaves me looking forward to the next visit.

I also love sitting at my father's feet listening just listening to him talk for he is filled with much wisdom concerning a lot of things. I respect his views on things whether I agree with him or not. I respect his views because right or wrong there is always a bit of wisdom to be found.

While I was pondering on all of this and my Father, I thought of God, Jesus, and how much they love me. I admire God for sending Jesus, and Jesus who died on the cross for my sins. He gave up all his glory to come to earth just so we might all go to Heaven and live.

I thought of the verse in the bible that says in 2 Corinthians 5:8, "We are confident, yes, well pleased rather to be absent from the body and to be present with the Lord." In Isaiah 57:1, it goes on to say, the righteous man who dies "Is taken away from evil, he enters into peace."

To be absent from the body is to be present with the Lord. I thought of how nice it would be to hug Jesus. To hold him, and to feel loved, and protected. To not only live in Heaven but sharing Heaven with Jesus while basking in his peace and feeling his love. With Jesus, I will have all of eternity to hug him.

Some day as sad as it is, I will no longer be able to hug my precious father here on earth anymore. One day here on Earth, my children will not be able to hug me or their father anymore. That is just how life and death is, but I will get to look forward to hugging Jesus when I leave this body, and it will feel like all the pleasant feelings I felt while hugging my earthly father, only it will be a trillion times better, and I will have all of eternity to hug him in all of Heavens glory. I will be able to share all this with my earthly father, along with countless family and friends.

You too can have all of what Jesus provides if you make the decision to let him into your heart. My prayer for you is that you make the decision to find peace in a relationship with Jesus.

PEACE THROUGH THE NIGHTMARE

I was alone and walking down the street. It was lined with quaint little shops with striped awnings over the windows. It was in the middle of the day and the weather was fair. I was not sure exactly what it was I was looking for. I went in and out of the stores like I was searching for something, and I felt anxious, but over what I did not know. As I was looking down the street deciding what store to go into next, I saw a woman with an aged looking face. Her hair was past her shoulders and was thick, fuzzy and wavy. Her chin jutted out just as much as her nose. At first, I did not think much of her except I noticed she was a bit on the scary looking side which frightened me. If this had been a television movie I would have shut it off. But it was a bad dream.

It did not take long before I noticed that she began to follow me from store to store. I did not feel threatened or fearful at first. It was daytime, I was not paying her much attention and she did not seem like much of a threat to me at the time. However, I soon noticed she knew what store I was going to go in and she did her best to go into the store just before me. I did not know what this woman was doing, but it seemed when she went in the stores before me, the owners of that same store would not let me enter after her. I would ask the store owners why they refused me entrance to their store, yet I got no answer. I continued to try to enter every store but as I quickly found out the strange woman had already been there and was telling the owners something negative about me that swayed the owners into refusing my entrance into their store. It was obvious the woman did not like me and was spreading ugly rumors about me everywhere I tried to go. I had no idea why this woman did not like me or why she was out to get me. I began to feel an eerie feeling and I could feel the fear beginning to rise. By now the woman felt like a real threat to me. Now she was causing me great strife, fear, and great uncertainty.

She was attacking my character and it seemed like she was out to destroy me but I did NOT know her. I searched myself from inside out trying to come to terms with the lady's attempt to cause me great distress. I tried to figure out if I had done something to deserve her attempts to ruin me, yet I could find none. I did not even know this woman, yet she knew me, and she had set out to destroy a part of my life. Would she succeed?

While this dream or vision I had, contained a message of some kind, and even though I did not yet understand what that message was, I kept it stored away in the back of my mind. If I ever saw the woman with the blond hair and jutted chin I would have no other choice than to run from her as quick as I could. The more I remembered about her from the dream, the more I wanted to stay away from her at any cost if I ever really saw her. All she wanted was to discredit and disgrace me. This is what Satan wants to do to each one of us. I had no revelation in this matter or the woman, who like the devil, had tried to destroy me.

The bible tells us the devil, much like a lion, roams around seeking whom he may destroy. He can do this by using others in our life, or by using situations we find ourselves in. Sometimes he tries to destroy our peace of mind by using others who try being a judge, handing out a guilty verdict in anything we do. In doing so, we may fall prey to their judgment. We ourselves sometimes judge others, not realizing we are hurting those we judge. There is only one rightful judge, and that is Jesus.

We are told in Matthew 7:1, "Judge not, that ye be not judged. For with what judgement ye judge, ye shall be judged." However, Jesus is not saying we can't distinguish between right or wrong, because sin is sin no matter what situation you may be in. He is saying we should not judge someone for their sin because we sin just as well. When Jesus judges he does so in his omniscience. We should allow Jesus to be the judge. Psalm 75:7, "But God is the judge; He puts down one and exalts another..." Romans chapter 2 tells how we judge others for what we see, yet we do the same things they do.

Let's allow God to judge others. And while this dream in some respect came to pass, Jesus was there with me through it all. No matter what, I will always have Jesus.

THE PERSISTENT ONE

My daughter is a kindhearted young woman, but none the less subject to human nature as we all are. She is not one easily moved by emotions unless it is some matter of serious consequence. We have a dearly loved small Rat Terrier weighing in at a whopping 5 or 6 pounds. She has been in our family since she was five weeks old and that was 16 years ago. She has moved with our family two times to new homes to which she quickly adjusted to. She was in the car with us when it crashed. The crash was serious enough that we were told it could have easily cost our son's life. We were all in seat belts except for Queenie. She had been lying next to me. She survived the crash but became lost at the accident sight due to the many lights of emergency vehicles having scared her. It was a miracle she survived. She was missing for three days before she was found and that was by the grace of God.

She met all twelve of our grandchildren. She celebrated with us in family marriages and mourned with us through divorces. She was with us when we unexpectantly lost our precious daughter in law who went to be with the Lord. Queenie comforted me as I fought cancer, and she never protested when we rescued other dogs in need of a home.

Yes, Queenie is quite a dog. Maybe that is why we try to have such a great deal of patience with her in her old age. It takes much patience to endure the times she strictly demands certain things.

For instance, each night without fail Queenie comes as my daughter sits in her chair at night. She sits right in front of my daughter and stares at her. If there is no response Queenie will begin to bark loudly without stopping. My daughter may be deeply involved in a television show, or just not feeling well but no matter what, Queenie will bark for several minutes, and we are convinced she would go on for hours, if we did not respond to her demands and wishes.

Whether we are busy or not, when we can stand her barking no longer my daughter will patiently get up and get Queenie whatever she likes. Make no bones about it, if you do not get her what she wants the first time she asks or demands, she will stare you down and bark until someone gets up and gets her what she wants. Only after she gets what she wants will she lie down satisfied.

In the bible there is a story about the persistent woman and a judge which is found in Luke 18:1-8. I believe It is written about to tell us to not give up. The woman kept going to the judge demanding justice. The judge tried to ignore her, but she kept coming back until the judge got tired of her and gave her what she wanted. Like this woman we should go to God in prayer about every situation and not give up.

How bad do you want it? The salvation of a loved one? Guidance from the Lord in a certain matter? A marriage on the rocks that only the Lord can save? Seeking to get back a lost relationship from a close and beloved family member? I could go on for an awfully long time suggesting areas you may need help with.

If an old dog can get a young woman to drop what she is doing and get whatever the dog wants by barking at her consistently, the dog has learned to be persistent. Without a doubt when speaking of the one and only God of the whole universe, who sent his only begotten son to die on the cross for our sins because he loves us, makes it easy to believe that if we desire his help we need only to be determined to pray the situation through until the end. God our father is much higher than a dog, and any judge that ever walked the face of the Earth. He has more love for us than we could ever have for a dog or a human. If a judge gives into someone because they are persistent and they recognize that only he can help, than how much more so will our heavenly father give to us the children he loves because of our recognizing his divine ability to do the impossible.

Today whatever your need is my friend, I know the place to go. It is to the throne of grace, where our Heavenly father, and our Lord and Savior sit watching over our every move, every day, willing and able to meet our every need. YOU HAVE NOT BECAUSE YOU ASK NOT. James 4:2-3.

I SAW THE LIGHT

I was on my knees praying in front of the window where the sun could shine down directly on me landing on my face. I was praying with my eyes closed, yet I could still see the light coming from the sun. I felt so close to the Lord, on my knees in prayer. I felt at peace, warm, and in touch with the Lord. I could have stayed like that forever. I never wanted the moment to end.

As I was praying it suddenly got dark. I opened my eyes hoping to see the light, but the sun had gone behind the clouds. It was still light outside, but not near as bright as it had been when the sun was out. I continued to pray and eventually noticed it getting brighter with the sun coming out of the clouds. I was once again enjoying the light and warmth as I prayed.

The experience I had just been through reminded me of something Jesus had said in the bible. Jesus clearly states he is the Light of the world. {John 9:5} Even in the darkest times there is still that ray of light and hope in Jesus. If we follow Jesus, we will walk in his light and not in darkness. {John 8:12} The light of the Lord never leaves us even when life seems to be at its darkest. Jesus is and always will be our ray of light.

And when our work here on Earth is finally done, and our bodies grow tired of life here on Earth, Jesus still encourages us not to fear. Psalm 23:4 "Yea though I walk through the valley of the shadow of death, I will fear no evil: for thou art with me; thy rod and thy staff they comfort me."

OUT OF THE DEPTHS I CRY

One afternoon after having a somewhat stressful day, I had gone into my prayer room to get away from it all and to spend time in prayer with Jesus. While praying I heard one of my fur babies crying right outside the door. I could hear her breathing and moving as close as she could to the door. I knew she wanted to come in the room with me and play as we kept her toys in the prayer room as well.

Despite hearing her cries which were getting louder and more desperate, I told myself I was going to ignore her and continue praying. However, when her cries became even more desperate sounding, and oh so sincere, I felt myself wanting to let her in with me so she would not be sad anymore. And that is exactly what I did. I let her in with me because I love her. I did not want her to be sad and to cry anymore, nor did I want to ignore her. When she came into the room, she immediately grabbed one of her toys and brought it to me. I threw the toy and she ran happily after it, not wanting it to get to far away from her. I laughed as she shook the stuffing's out of the toy. Good thing that toy was not real.

God loves us. He never ignores us or is too busy for us. He is with us day in and day out. His love causes mercy and grace to be with us every day of our lives. We owe everything to God. We have a good God. Once we accept him into our heart, we long to be in his presence. We can hear his voice by reading his word, the bible. This is just one of the ways he speaks to us.

Listen closely. Can you hear his voice? He is but a whisper away. If you spend time in your bible you are spending time with him. If you spend time in prayer you are spending time with him. His love covers you and guides you.

There is a wonderful verse in the bible found in Psalms 130:1, "Out of the depths I cry to you, oh Lord. Lord hear my voice: hear my cries for mercy. I wait for the Lord. My soul waits for the Lord." When everything seems to be going wrong, you can cry out to Jesus, from the depths of despair, and you can know without a doubt he is listening, ready to act in your behalf.

REMAINING FATHFUL

When I go into my prayer room at home it is with the intention of spending time alone with God. One day my husband, my daughter, and myself were busy getting ready for the winter storm that was approaching. Also, I had my husband's upcoming back surgery on my mind. I was not looking forward to his upcoming surgery, but I did not want him to be in pain either, so the surgery was necessary. I was also genuinely concerned about all the time he needed off from his job for surgery. It would be without pay the whole time he was recovering. I had a difficult time sitting still for more than a minute without my mind wandering off to one of the areas that I was concerned about. I needed to find a job and I needed to find it real fast.

Also, while I was trying to pray there were even more distractions. I could hear the shrill barking of my dog outside my door. I wanted to relax, and one of the ways for me to do that, was to cuddle the dog that was barking and tenderly caress her fur. This almost always calmed me down in a short period of time.

Despite all the distractions all around me, I just wanted to pray. The cares of the world were closing in on me it seemed. The bible in Mark 4:19, talks about not letting the things of the world get in the way of our following Jesus and spending time with him. It says, "And the cares of this world, and the deceitfulness of riches, and the lusts of other things entering in, choke the word, and it becometh unfruitful." In other words, sometimes the worries of this life, and the desire for other things come in and choke the word making it cease to bear fruit.

Trusting in God may not always be easy whenever we find ourselves in a bad situation, but we can be assured that we have a God who cares about what we are going through. If you find yourself in a difficult situation that seems impossible to get out of, pray. You will see God working in your life in ways you never thought possible.

BROKEN LIVES

There was a broken light in the bathroom, and it needed to be fixed right away. Of course, we were out of light bulbs which meant on this cold and rainy night, I would have to go to the store and purchase some. I would rather sit at home with my husband and daughter watching TV, but that would not be getting the light bulbs we needed so I had no choice but to go to the store.

Once you put the light bulb in you simply reach for the light switch and you have light. Once you reach out to Jesus, he sheds light into our lives. In John 8:12 we read that Jesus is the light of the world. If we make Jesus our Lord and Savior, we will forever walk in his light.

We should not be afraid to ask for his help. He is waiting for us to acknowledge that we need his help. Simply ask him and he will shed new light into your life. Jesus comes in fixing a situation and the light of the Lord fills your heart and life. Wouldn't you rather be in the light? Please do not delay in asking Jesus to help. The longer you wait, is just more time for you to go without the blessing of having things working in your life. Jesus wants to bless you. Won't you let him into your heart? All you or anyone else need to do is to ask. I myself have asked Jesus into my heart as a child, and though now I am considered a senior citizen, I have never for one moment regretted making that decision to ask Jesus into my heart.

BLESSING THE BEATEN DOWN

I have been blessed to be able to get a firsthand demonstration of what the bible may be referring to when in Luke 10:25-37. It speaks of helping our brother in need. Our granddaughter who is the medical field while driving home noticed a man standing on the street corner holding a sign. She felt she was to busy to stop but after feeling led to do so, she did end up stopping and talking with the man. She allowed the man to tell of his situation. She then after getting his permission, prayed over him, regarding the things he needed in his life. An interesting thing he told her was that although he had been there on the corner with his sign, she was only the second person in two days to stop.

That could have been one of the reasons the people in the bible did not help the traveler despite his having been beaten and robbed. Maybe they were to busy to stop, or since the traveler was one of their enemies, they felt no need to stop for someone they despised.

Jesus looked past the fact that the traveler was in a region where he would be despised. The good Samaritan, also looked past their social status, and felt compelled to stop and help the man. Our granddaughter looked past the young man standing on the street corner. Just as most people would not stop for the traveler in the bible, and only two people stopping in two days to help this man on the street corner, what can the moral of this story in today's setting be?

Could it be that Jesus is asking us to see the traveler and the beggar as he sees them? Could Jesus be wanting us to see these people as well as our enemies, as our neighbor? The Jews and Samaritans were enemies, yet the Samaritan took the time to help the Jewish traveler. Have we ever noticed someone standing on the corner, holding a sign, asking for help? Did we stop to help, or did we pass them by due to our being to busy to stop? What is God asking us to do in this situation? The answer is found in Luke Chapter ten.

As humans we may be responsible at one time or another for having feelings of wanting to get even with or taking revenge on people that are not like us. Jesus helped the traveler knowing the traveler was seen as the enemy. He knew he could go out of his way to help, and though he helped the traveler, the traveler could still end up hating Jesus. But, the good Samaritan helped the traveler anyway. Can we do as Jesus did? Can we help someone in need regardless of what social status they are in, or what race they may be, or what country they may be from? Jesus helped us yet while we were sinners. Romans 5:8 tells us how God demonstrated his love for us by dying on the cross for us while we still sinners.

By taking the time to stop and help this beggar on the street corner, our granddaughter helped without expecting something in return for her helping. Our world might be better off if we could be like the good Samaritan, or our granddaughter, by doing little acts of kindness. What would our world be like if we were to show more empathy for our fellow man?

Perhaps we could spend time reading about the good Samaritan and the Jewish traveler and come to a Godly decision in taking time to help our fellow man when we see them in need.

I for one am totally blessed by Jesus laying down his life for all of mankind and myself while we were still sinners. Jesus took the time to help us regardless of our status on Earth. I hope you too will see how much Jesus must love us, in that he laid down his life for us. He wants us to be a part of Heaven forever. He even makes us mansions to live in for an eternity in Heaven. John 14:2 explains how Jesus has prepared many mansions for us, if we place our trust in him. No matter what your status is here on Earth, you will be accepted by Jesus, if you only ask him to come into your heart. You will not be sorry.

Printed in the United States
By Bookmasters